To the version of you who needed to hear this
— pain was never your ending, but only the beginning of your rebirth.

red flags

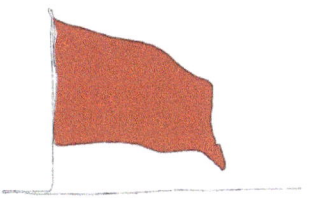

There you stood, my twin flame waving a flag that looked crisp white from a distance.

Each step closer revealed the flag-stained red.

The journey to you was long, but you allowed your battles before me to bleed you dry as the drops blemished your flag.

Your flag wasn't a case of surrender, it was a warning.

I didn't invest in myself enough before meeting you.

If I had, our relationship would have soared into beauty instead of crashing into flames.

I knew no boundaries for myself.

I can no longer play victim to being a hopeless romantic.

The universe was just vibrating off my frequency.

Looking for acceptance from people who don't care about you is equivalent to trying to wear a pair of shoes that won't fit. If you keep trying, you're asking for pain, rejection, and wounds bound to open. It comes with sex, empty promises, broken trusts, accusations, and emotional abuse, sometimes physical abuse.

Nothing good comes from it, but sweet spoken words and actions remain absent. "It" does and says just enough to keep you around. For a couple of days or weeks, you are the queen that you indeed are, and then once you are hooked, everything goes back to how it was. "It" refuses to be honest with you. "It" lingers around you for its selfish reasons, which is to drain you of the "it" you possess inside of you. It is that complicated, back-and-forth, inconsistent passion that drives you insane. It causes you to lose yourself by trying to give and give constantly. It takes without considering how you may feel and doesn't think twice about giving.

Excuses, excuses, excuses are all you are stuck with. Questions bat your mind as to whether this person truly cares for you or not. "It" leaves you alone when you need love the most but returns void yet feening for more of your honesty, cares, concerns, and loyalty only to devour you leaving you to feel belittled, not good enough. It doesn't know what it could be, how beautiful it could become. It causes many consequences and confusion when the game is over. It has its repercussions when you love someone who doesn't love themselves.

So you're asking yourselves what is "IT"?

    Inexpensive IT

You can be compatible with someone by trauma too;

        it's not always love.

Can we exist any other way?
To not be bonded to one another by the depths of our love and the shallows of our flaws that ever so often escapes us.
Flaws continue to rise as if it were heat, burying our love into a burrowing abyss so deep.
Love becomes so dark, our eyes can't adjust.
Flaws become so hot that it burns us.

We don't spit love, we spit fire.

        two raging dragons dancing in a circle

My light shines bright in my eyes. Eager to love through my light, I surround myself around those who act as if my light is dim. Without doubt, my light begins to flicker. Now I'm the flickering light that needs tightening. I can last for a lifetime, but your attention is on the light that lasts less than 3 months. Sure it shines bright, but it burns quicker, then you're out looking for another.

I guess it's harder to notice that my light only needed a quick turn to the right to last that lifetime that you so desperately needed.

    centennial light

He refused to tell the truth giving me a choice of pills red or blue.

Red is what we know of passion, love, courage, and strength. Taking a look from the lesser end of his choice it's filled with rage, malice, stress, lust, and impulse.

Blue is what we remember to be trusting, stable, loyal, and faithful. When I asked him for the truth expecting a hard pill to swallow of honesty blue, without thought he shoved down my throat the pill of the lesser end of the bloody hue.

The twinkle he left in my eye turned to dust as he wasn't strong enough to resist the yearnings of lust. To honor our love by giving me the blue pill may have been ill, but I wouldn't be at this stand still. Either way it's a lose lose. The greatest ruse I've given myself is knowing you were my muse.

I took you back with ease each time.

It isn't the past humiliation that bothers me, it's knowing I'm still disrespecting myself by still being with you,

    even with forgiveness.

The tears I've cried, this pain that has yet to die. These feelings that I'm feeling aren't even mine. The moment you laid with her, you gave her a portion of our soul tie.

I lost sense of myself, wondering why.

A place in her bed where I'll never physically step, is where my power lies.

I've given my power to people freely without thought.
I left my power in certain places I've lived and once I visited,

I felt helpless.

The problem isn't that she didn't know her worth,

    the problem is she was waiting

               for them to notice.

It was hard to let go of the fantasy of you,
of us,
which made it harder to actually let go of us.

One look at you and everything was vibrant, everything so beautiful you were made in diamonds. Mesmerized by the image I captured so vividly in my heart, your confession to stop painting you rose gold was becoming so clear, I'd have to restart. You began to tell the truth of the real you and my version of you is incorrect.

You're not rose gold, you are but they're just specks. You show and tell me to look at the real you and once I do, I'll see you'll never be the rose gold painting I created you to be. The more I stopped painting and strip you, my creation, the more I lose you and that's something I cannot face.

I have to strip you down from what I see and realize the real you is someone I can't keep in my place. I keep thinking if I hold on to my version of you, I get to keep my painting.

I have to let you go, see you can't fit into my world so I release you and pray that one day you actually shine rose gold.

Scrolling through my contacts to find the right call is a substitute from not being able to call you.

I stayed in toxic overdue relationships due to attachment issues. I noticed these attachment issues stemmed from my abandonment issues. While dealing with these abandonment issues, I made an invisible vow to be validated from others. I would always ask myself why can't they see me. It wasn't until I cried and begged my lover "I just want to be seen and heard by you." His reply "I do."

I was seeking validation. I wanted a pat on the back for being the good girlfriend. I wanted a congratulations for completing college and figuring out motherhood with mother and father wounds. I wanted to be saved by someone that loves me the way I love. I loved hard because I yearned to be loved properly by others. Not knowing I had to put in the work to love myself the way I desired.

I'm not his dream girl
I'm the girl of his one time dream
He tries to chase that same dream like he's trying to find his first high.

I'm not his ideal girl
I'm the girl he sees and gets a glimpse of a life that is ideal

I'm not the girl he wants
I'm the girl that he wants to need, that itch he scratches for but can never reach

I'm always three steps ahead, three because one, two steps gives him a chance to touch me and with one more he's caught up, and once he does I become a blur.

I'm too close to see for the farsighted that tries to see near.

I'm too right for the guy that's left.
Left behind while chasing fantasies and lust.

Sometimes a person can only see your growth just as much as they have grown.

Understand that there are people who refuse to see you just to make themselves feel better about who they are.

raveled

There is a place where I hold you responsible for this pain that I have carried.

The emotional turmoil, my issues.

They are baggage that I carry with my relationship with my significant other.

The inner child remains unhealed

    unhealed

With crying eyes,

lying lips, and dying love

what is a relationship?

I'm in love with your tranquility,

your chaos,

your light,

your darkness.

It's the imbalance within you that draws me near,

which makes me question...

Am I not stable too?

Hear yourself overflowing with words to fill another.

Like glassware, we are made fragile.

One wrong drop of word, we shatter.

glass figures

Imagine sitting in a room alone, full of discomfort.

My feelings exact.

I'm not at home in my own body

speaking MY ANGER tells you I love ME.

speaking MY SOUL tells you I love YOU.

I visited the place I grew up.

The building was vacant and dark.

Not even much as a speck of light.

I realized from that moment forward, it was only myself in this fight.

No home, nobody

deception, envy, rage, doubt, unworthy, and abandonment of self and others.

all are stored in my collection cabinet. every once in a while, I polish them as they are the items of what I define as beauty.

each time I polish them, the Universe serves me another trophy to add to my collection

after all it is what I worked hard to achieve.

The day I showed you my deepest scars,

my reasoning for a trampled foundation.

You reply with "I can't compete with that"

"I can't compete with that" was your way of telling me

    I need to love myself.

What frightens me the most is a life without you.
To go without you would be driving to an unknown destination without cease. Nothing would make sense without you. I have a part of you that will always remain with me.
I wouldn't live without your full presence.

I would be merely existing.

I once had the opportunity to decide to love someone through their lost times of life or to leave and allow them to discover who they truly are. It was a time full of difficulty with the person I loved dearly, no matter the conditions. I would travel through mountains and the lake of fire to stand by their side. That's how strong my love stood for that person. Inevitably, I was drawn to their tranquility as well as their chaos...

Toxic? Probably.

I didn't see it that way. It was love. Unconditional love. I didn't know what I thought was unconditional love would slowly kill me. Trying to survive during the darkest times would drain me of my individuality. Love and time were no longer by my side. I lost myself to this person, without them noticing, nor myself. Their love was venomous yet pleasurable.

Addicted? Maybe.

The thought of refusing to leave initially came from not finding anyone better, and losing the little bit of happiness I did receive. On the other hand, the thought of refusing to leave came from not wanting to abandon him. Fast forward, I can picture myself not regretting to leave, to save myself.
The most burdensome question remains......

In a world of choices, when will I choose me?

Hello

I'm very familiar to almost everyone in the world. I love to make the mind second guess things. When people discover their happiness, I'm that small voice whispering pessimistic things in their ear.

My main goal is vacillation.

I'm the reason your girlfriend questions you about things that you could be possibly lying about. I'm the reason you can't trust females because of what your first love did to you.

You recall the day she left you, without a care in the world. You play this scene over and over again until you've built up wall, and you won't dare trample the bricks.

I'm the native form of depression and anxiety. And oh, do I love it when you feed into me and amplify my existence.

Paranoia lingers throughout your mind, soul, and spirit.

I will not go away because you want to feel me and sometimes you need me as an excuse to display the fear you have. You blame me when it should be you blaming yourself for not wantingto let go of the past.

I may be the reason you ruin your next relationship with anyone. You're inferior to everyone that is not you. You feel as if the next person is more beautiful or just better at being a human than you are...when the truth is the next person faces their wrath with me, they just conceal it better than you.

I laugh at you. You allow me to belittle you and the beauty of me is no one can see me unless you reveal me to them. Maybe one day you will learn to defeat me but until then I'm here to stay causing you to be envious and whatnot of the next person while you feel like shit.

The day you defeat me is the day I will no longer be a nuisance to you. That day will be up to you, until then, I reign.

You think I can't live without you,

I can.

My world is much better with you in it. At least I think it is. I try to make sense of the inconsistency that exists in what we have as more questions arise. How many times have we broken up and to make up? It's too many times to count on my hands, so I try stretch my brain to remember each moment we've argued and drifted away. The more we do this, the more I began to think what if the universe is telling me that my life will be better without you in it. It'll be hard at first, but as the days past and the more I dig to search for myself, the easier it will be.

I'm starting to believe I'm better off with you now, and once you see that you'll come back and we'll start over again for the 20th time...

repeated cycles

I begin to watch the movie while occupied. At work. At class. In the gym. Anywhere. I think about leaving my current destination just to lay in bed and playback every disappointing moment that you played a part of in our movie. My heart tears a bit each time. I press pause on the text messages and the likes on social media as I trance out only to rewind them.

Play.

Now it is recorded in my memory. Seeing you break what is yours is like my favorite, unsatisfying movie. I rewind to the times that were great. Only to fast forward to the now of thinking why can't you see me. I'm am it. I am the chosen one. The best. The person that defines what you are. You're so blinded of the lies that were blatantly exposed to you. She is not your destiny. She was the lie of your life. I am the candor. I'm your now and forever. She is the distortion of your past.

I begin to feel that you like the older version of your movie over the new one. The old version was an illusion. Everything was perfect. It was perfect because it wasn't real. You were bamboozled my dear.

The new version is too real for you...this movie brings you into your manhood. It is time to lay those boyish fantasies to rest. It's imperfect but you are wiser than you once were. This is better for you. I am your destiny.

Play.

Now we find ourselves distant, unable to break the cycle of the distrust and deceit that you've created. You find a new one that is entertaining. I watch as you destroy your present as well as your future with me. You have jeopardized your family for the attention of what you believe to be better than what you have now. Only to be left alone and dissatisfied of your present because of your decisions. Rewind back to the scene where I found panties in your bag, only to discover they do not belong me.

Play

I can never understand how you can tell me I'm more than good enough and I'm all that you desire.

Only to leave me permanently to entertain your soul temporarily.

the settle

you were painted so beautifully on that blank canvas. Just the thought of you igniting the room and everyone gushing over you sparked the thrill in me

(settling for the one I created in my mind).

dipping your hand into another cookie jar because it looked good from your staring. only to devour the cookie that is not mine with ease. dazzled in sprinkles, I became aware of your hand taking its pleasures in the other jar as you left a trail back to mine

(settling for non-mutual respect).

no matter how close I get to entering the lake, the further it seems to drift. my thoughts of the lake lighting with magnificence of iridescent hues are something to dream of. Only to dip my foot and realize not much has changed from above

(settling: ignoring gut instinct).

Things may appear to have changed, but underneath lies the same.

There's no me and you. There's just me and then, there's just you.

I fear that you will truly fall in love with someone that is not me. I fear that you will see in them what you could not see in me. I fear that you won't remember me as I begin to fade from your life. I fear that I didn't mark your heart and mind with my spirit just as you marked mine. I fear not having you, because there is no other you to have.

I fear these feelings and I hurt for you;
       my mouth will scream I HATE YOU!!
           .... but my heart whispers I love you.

itching for a swallow of your water offerings.
refreshing at first, later revealing a taste of my dislike.
a tang of bitterness left on the tip of my tongue, switching the glass only to
endure the same bitterness lying on the tip of my tongue
as you remain present in other lovers.

cottonmouth

is it knowing you can imagine but never actually grasp?

is it knowing that you can fantasize because its more exciting than reality?

is it because she is someone to always wonder about?

the unknown gives you a rush. versus when you're with me it is the known, the familiar you use as a crutch.

intrigued with what's not yours, bored with what is.

hitting that follow button for your blast from the past stirs up many thoughts. when you follow, I know the double tap comes right after, burning me with insecurity and emotions left hollow.

double tap

In hopes that we would share the same language of love, I stayed. Physically we understood each other, mentally and emotionally occasionally. Even your spirit spoke different.

I decided to translate my spirit as you translated yours. Unknowingly, weeks became years as we reside on separate pages, speaking in different tongues. Our spirits vibrating at different frequencies.
Our love language is nonexistent.
As the years pass, the truth began to unveil itself. Suddenly the glass wasn't so rose colored.
There was no longer a sigh of relief.
I remember when my lungs filled themselves with joy and warmth, back when I could smell the fresh country scents, enjoy the quiet, watching the sunset orange yellow.

Now, it feels like a haunting.

Sunsets are no longer.

Everything is just as colored as dramatic cool hue.

A dampened blue.

In the thick quiet, I hear the fights, I could feel the lonesomeness. Like an abandoned house thatremembers the imprints of feet basing its frame, the creaking floorboards are a trigger of every wail of the tears I've cried. I think of the wondering of the late nights, the not so white lies.
The love is silent, the memories deafening.

It's too loud. I can't hear my own thoughts. Somebody please makes this stop. I can no longer smell the country scents. The stench of lies buys out the scent of the countryside.

Once I realized the importance of my spirit my energy, I gained my power back. My spirit had to retreat to save itself from you. I would rather face the torture from the withdrawals of you, than to have live through the fucked-up pleasures going the wrong way on a one-way street.

I can no longer give when you are not giving.

I can no longer give when I'm not receiving.

But yet I find myself ascending with my hand reaching backwards, waiting for you to take holdas I'm drowning into an abyss.
We will never speak the same language as long as we're on different frequencies.

    frequency discrepancy

Our love is like a photo, still.

Locked away in a book of memories that we haven't touched in years.

Our memories dull, like a picture overtime.

Fading.

Let's take a glimpse of the past, before this picture vanishes.

polaroid

Thirsting for water, so that I may bloom.

Molding myself into becoming my own.

The many obstacles that come to pass while evolving into a woman.

The daily battles,
the inner turmoil,
the caged, ravenous beast that remains unheard.

While her life remains salt less, the woman inside remains unheard.

unheard I

My love, my sweet.

My pain, my pleasure

I give you permission to break my heart.

I choose you. I've chosen you time and time again, and I will forever choose you. You brighten my days like the sun after the rain.

You are my sun and my rain.

You strengthen my spirits yet you weaken them at the same time.

How is that possible?

For as long as you been mine,

I've been searching for a certain love, for years it's been missing.

It has taken multiple arguments of the same subject to discover that it is I who can give that certain love that I've been exploring for.

Only I can comply I.

So many people love conditionally because they are not sure of themselves.

Love may exist right now because of the need for it or the lack of love within self. He can't love himself because he doesn't know how. He goes searching...inquest of something only he thinks a woman can provide for him. But her love isn't enough for him. He goes to the next one searching for the same, still unsatisfied with the next. He takes you, you, you, and her too. Taking from all of you, leaving you empty and restless while giving nothing in return.

Your love is of convenience. His conditional love will not last simply because he loves on a condition. Do you know how easy it is to give up with that type of love when there is always a because that follows behind the reasoning for his love for you? With that, follows what he receives from you. There are never talks of giving as he doesn't intend to give anything except sex and lies. Everything is for his benefit, though it may seem like you're getting something in return...you're not.

When are you going to realize your worth? When will you realize that he's the one that's damaged goods and that you cannot fix him? When you realize that's its past due to walk away?

That woman inside crying aloud to be set free screams as her throat is filled with excruciating pain her voice is nearly faint, "Un tame me! Release me!!!" Uncertain that if she is released, will she come to terms of loving herself or will she see a reflection of hate. Aware that her inner being must take the spotlight eventually, hesitation ponders.

Doubt and fear consume her from alleviation. Days become years as her garrulous ego still lingers. Continuing life with the mindset of what she is not, she has filled herself with lies and self-deceit

.... that dying woman inside of her remains lying to her death as she knows she is not living but merely existing. Everything is of bore as the blame is placed into the reasoning of her life, without thought of the blame being placed on herself.

While her life remains salt less, the woman inside remains unheard.

unheard II

Dying to be free

I have 3 ball and chains tied to the shaft of my ankles I have the key, but I haven't put it to use.

I carry the dead weight of my loved ones that were supposed stay.

My every thought of trying to rationalize their exit adds 5 pounds to the weights each time I think about it.

That's 5 pounds from 3 people too many.

Instead of using the key to free myself, I hold the key tightly to my chest, while the ball and chains are still attached to my ankles in hopes that those 3 will return ready to accept my love and release me from the shackles themselves.

for the boy that knows no love, when love comes to visit him, anxiety and fear follows. love is a stranger, something that only exists in fantasies. lost boy searches for himself in the thighs and heads of many giving himself up to that and plenty. attention and stroking of the ego are the fuel, being seen by others is the match. the fire is lit just as fast as it dies. everything is coal. lost boy stands there with nothing but an empty soul.

lost boy

Coasting. The long rides. The timeless talks.

Coinciding on the same page. All is well. You love all of me. IM PERFECT in all caps for imperfections is what you tell me. The phrase "After the rain" doesn't exist, when we're together. we are two suns becoming one, cursing the rain afar. There's no storm to weather. Rather than sweet nothings, candied somethings are the regular. Fast car, all I see is green for GO, but little did I know....

Love bombing at its finest. Thinking I've met my match, but you rock bottomed me as if you were a wrestler.

Protagonist vs. Antagonist.

My flaws begin to backfire from I'm perfect to me being a wreck. The protagonist becoming the #1 reason for your unhappiness. The sweet nothings became the regular as there was nothing sweet about our now regulars. I'm the blame for your concealed fault. The timeless talks became talks of the time we spent less. Jumping to different chapters in our book, I'm on page 28, you're on 30, when were supposed to be on 29, we can't relate. Splitting our sun into two so you can outshine me, I guess cursing the rain was a joke because I've cried many tsunamis.

We reside at this light with your feet on the brake. Stop and go, stop and go with my head jerking back and forth you're starting to give me a headache. Stop and go, stop and go, like the gas is running low.

STOP!

I look to you to see how long before you take your foot off the brake so WE can go. Or maybe, I should get out of the car and just go.

Gaslighting

therapy

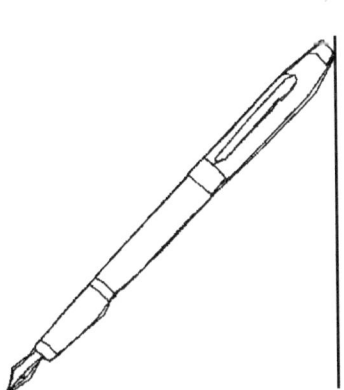

my therapist asked me to describe a relationship

between a narcissist and an empath.

I told her ego vs. soul

Your love felt familiar. ...

I've had it before, it was served from a different body.

The Universe is trying to tell me something.

I think I get it now.......

karmic attachments

My conversations with the brick wall are better.

I don't have to expect a response or changed actions.

I have a habit of collecting emotions

YOU CAN NOT TELL ME HOW TO EXPRESS

MY FREEDOM

underneath anger is the greatest lesson waiting to be taught.
There is life beyond the blind fury.

our spirits collided;

the mirror shattered cursed with 7 years of bad luck.

seven years of uncertainty, seven years of ups and downs.

seven years of knowing we weren't destined to be.

With our tethered cords attached firmly.

Tightly gripped as if we're bear trapped at our feet. the tethered cord lay rested in toxic black.

seven years pass, we begin to piece our mirror together, puzzling each shard of glass to fit intothe right space while cutting ourselves to fit it.

we come to thoughts of allowing the mirror to remain broken and walk away while we purchase a new mirror separate from one another.

Our mirror will always be known as broken as we know there is more work to be done. We fill our cracks with gold just as the Japanese.

we become twice as beautiful as our cracks show our struggles and pain.

We become unbreakable and beautiful from a broken mirror to a golden masterpiece for generations to tell, refusing to let our love die in vain.

mirrors

To be vocal, yet silenced

To speak loud, bold, with honesty with much pride, and still remain unheard.

God did not bless me with this tone that's anything but manual.

This tone goes on by auto.

This tone carries it's on motto.

I speak from the soul.

I speak from anger.

Neither are worth to ignore.

Conversations are like clothes, the mind a clothing basket.
Allowing dirty clothes to clutter the basket, one may become foul and messy.
With too many dirty clothes, the basket overflows and spews.

Sort and fold your clothes before placing them in your basket.

dirty laundry

You have to be certain of who you are.

People will come and go in your life and even still you have to remain sure of yourself.

With uncertainty comes insecurity.

I used to stare at other women and turn green, when in reality it was admiration behind the jealousy of other women's beauty.

I turned to comparison and picking out their flaws, meanwhile thinking she has it all.

I try to gain confidence about myself, as I stare at the mirror, I stand there wishing I wassomeone else.

All the while not loving myself.

They say beauty is in the eye of the beholder so it's me that I cannot see.

I have my father's eyes and my mother's smile.

Deep down I'm full of disgust, wishing I was someone else's child.

So, they could love me, and love me deep. Open minded is what they were not. Brain opposite of big, so that makes them closed minded and their train of thought small and petite.

I have my father's eyes and my mother's smile filled with self-hate. I want to be this and that just so they can congratulate....

Me.

All I can see is me. The me that I am not.

Outcast

Unfit

Too skinny, not thick. Me wishing that I was just like she.

She is fierce

She is bold

She is magic

She is gold

She is beauty that is overflowing with warmth, a heart not turned stone cold.

A walking goddess.

That was then.

Now, when I see a beautiful woman, I admire her beauty through love and compliments.

To gain confidence about myself, I choose to look inward and realize just how beautiful God made me, because I myself am a goddess.

I am beauty that is overflowing with warmth, a heart not turned stone cold.

I am gold.

I am magic.

I am bold.

I am fierce.

All I can see is me. The me that I am not. But no longer am I wishing that I was just like she.

How can I not love myself and admire my own inner and outer beauty?

There is only one me.

Boys choose pride over love.

If his actions aren't lining up with his words, he has chosen his ego over you.

There is a difference between focusing on the hurt creating your own suffering and living with the hurt, suffering.

When you wait for someone to be ready for you, it's not out of love that you're chosen.

You've been chosen out of default.

The Waiting Game

People that mistreat you, yet claim to love you do so out of fear and their personal issues.
Their words will tell they love you,
actions express you are the enemy.

lover's quarrel

Every person from my past I've crossed paths with has been a lesson.

"Thank you for sharing a portion of your spirit with me, it may not have been the best encounter, it may not have been the worst, and still, I thank you"

Every person in my present moment. "Thank you"

I realize people don't belong to me, we cross one another's path for a definitive reason and our purpose is fulfilled. I cannot remain selfish because that person is no longer in my life the way I would love for them to be. I can grieve and let go, but I cannot become resentful towards him orher.

People maneuver according to their own free will. If they have done something to you that has caused you hurt or suffering you will realize their actions, their choices have nothing to do with you. It's an internal conflict within themselves.

Each person you meet awakens a necessary growth that needs to transpire within you.
When we move forward in life, we take a piece of that person with us to our next chapter in life.

Silence the hatred, the anger, and the despair.

There is beauty behind the grief.

Anxiety is a sensitive wound that is too tender to bandage.

A lack of presence in the present.

Breath and return to the Now.

Friendship is a family created from the soul.

A platonic love that extends beyond the years of one's life.

Tying the knot of interchangeable energy.

The loyalty is phenomenal, the embracement is everlasting.

Love is forever formed and cherished.

This woman that was kept hidden for so long.

Buried deep within the trenches, beyond the darkness in the woods. Her strength was the number of countless men as she held her own during her darkest moments.

It was by her strength in the dark,

she shined.

She was zoned.

She was tired.

Carrying the roles of both man and woman.

She developed the persona of not needing a man.

I can only imagine a woman's son growing up seeing his mother as an "I'll do it myself" woman.

Yet, we wonder why our daughters grow up to be an "I'll do it myself" woman and the sons growup to be "She'll do it herself" men.

The son watched as his mom did things herself, allowing to dad to be lazy or absent. The son gets himself an "I'll do it myself" wife. Expecting that same masculinity from her as his mom embraced within herself. Little girls are birthed. The son turned man does the bare minimum with the girls, the house, just about anything that doesn't concern him solely. The girls see the wife maintaining everything. As the girls watched, they learned. The wife sees her daughters coming into their own, also becoming "I'll do it myself" children. They know not to depend on dad, but also refraining from bothering mom. The girls then grow up to become solely independent women. Both or one or the other will probably get married still holding the title as an "I'll do it myself" woman.

Do you recognize the wounded energy of femininity and masculinity?

A continuation of wounded femininity/masculinity generational curse in its own form.

I am Zuko birthed into the fire nation. Born from a mother forced to bow down and conjoin with a tyrant as my father.

With a heart filled with gold, my father tears me down, forces me into battle with him.

Burns me,

defeats me,

and banishes me to fulfill something of his desire.

While in search of his destiny, I lack vision of my own.

I see myself as Aang but I'm my own Ty Lee because I've blocked my own chi.

Without my chi, I'm just as blind as Toph when the burns scraped her feet.

I'm more like Zuko believing that my destiny of others is what is mine to hold.

The more I question the fire nation, more dirt begins to unfold.

Avatar America

Patience is waiting for a love that comes from your parents to come from a different body.

Uncertainty is the heart bound by rope.

The rope is pulled by both ends clinching the heart tighter making it harder to breath, making it harder to reach a decision.

Exhaustion is a continuous battle of accepting an undergrown love.

When the soul has reached beyond its limits, in a limitless space.

Constant crying and fighting for an undeserving love.

Learn to conserve your energy.

Rest is a breath of fresh air.

A break from earthly reality.

A clear mind, a clear heart.

A cleansing of the spirit.

No more wandering of any kind.

I picture myself reaching for the stars, but I can't quite grasp them.

I stretch my arms, making it harder to grasp, but once I pick myself up to stretch with my arms, touching the stars becomes easier.

The stars are hope.

Self-love is hugging your soul.

As I write, I am meditating, taking deep breaths.

As the stroke of my pen follows, I can feel the crisp fresh air trail down my airways into the pit of my stomach.

Awakening my spirit.

I tune out the distractions and listen to the surroundings closer.

I feel my heart beating at its own pace.

My body becomes as light as a feather.

I am more than this body.

My thoughts are clearer than they have ever been.

Light, warmth, love, smiles, and feels arouse from this body.

This is life.

meditation

Are we only here to share each other's spirit with one another to allow people to become better and to make the world better?

release

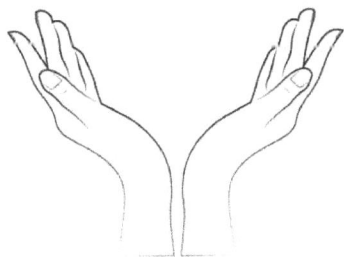

Words speak louder when my pen bleeds.

At the age of 25, I decided to sit down to have a chat with my inner child...

She stands there.....eyes big like the midnight owl, skinny petite, ponytails with yellow balls to act as a hair tie.

I can see her wearing a white collared shirt and navy-blue pants, her elementary school uniform. She looks lost and hopeless, but I know she's waiting for me.

I walk up to her confident, smiling, hoping to see her face change. I kneel down to her height as she gazes at me with her neck vertically stretched.

I smile.... "It's not your fault, people can only love you as much as they know how. Rejection is redirection and the path you've chosen has been good for the type of love you've been given. It's not your fault it's not you. You are loved wholly and deeply. The love you wantis in you."

I wiped her tears as I began to cry. We hugged ever so tightly, she tightly gripped me by my neck as her tears soaked my shirt and mine on hers.

I deeply exhale...

the healing begins....

                    heal

I've always needed glasses, even with the sight of 20/20. With my perfect vision, the world remained a blur. I was led by the blind with no hand to hold.

My vision narrowed and foggy. I was born into a family where my flavor was never given, stripped the moment mama pushed me out.

Deprived of self-trust, suffrage of spunk. house trapped to color within the lines.

28 years later, I purchased my glasses seeing myself for the very first time.

A pot roast for a stomach, elongated noodle like stretch marks and 2 soft dinner rolls on each side for love handles. My thighs dipped in honey while the back of them carry cellulose like pancakes while the batter is bubbling on the other side before flipping it over.

My breasts hang something like the cheese from an oven baked spaghetti with extra parmesan on top.

A full course meal.

Most people do not favor the full course meal. It's as if they question the ingredients of the recipe the Chef used.

enjoy!

I am everything that is beautiful. I am everything that is not.

I am beautifully flawed, an incomplete being.

Don't mind me if I became distant...

I choose to have my deepest talks with the moon.

I turn to my journal and notes to pen down my burdens, my joys, my thoughts.

I stare into the night sky and feel the vibrations of the full moon beginning to arise.

I listen to my inner being as peace overwhelms me; tranquility is the tone that is set for the remaining night.

I think of my lover.

I think of my offspring.

I think of my present breath.

I think of my ancestors and their current presence in the now.

I think of my craft.

Gratitude has entered.

The red/yellow skies become dim. All is quiet now.

The beauty that lies in the deep blue hues of the sky, nothing can surpass the moment.

blue hour

My greatest fear is to lose you,

but the universe reminded me that

I can never lose what was aligned for me.

I soar beyond this atmosphere.

I turn glitter in gold.

Fantasy into reality.

Nightmares into dreams.

Dreams into actuality.

Alchemy at its finest

Birthed from a mountain, the river flows along the likings of the created path. Rushing wildly, and calm but forever flowing.

Side by side, I stand with you as you flow your own path.

I can't see who is further down ready to take a sip of your offerings.

Worried for this beautiful river?

Yes.

For it is harder to keep the river clean as it is easier to pollute it with the works of this world.

You will come across others who will admire your current. I can't trail you forever.

So, I place blessings upon you that one day, your flow will lead you to an ocean,

      the body of freedom.

river child

A woman's wrath after being put through hell and back.

We leave behind damaged goods that were meant to be destroyed; they serve no use for us as werebuild anew.

After destruction, comes the reign of beauty.

hurricanes

There's power there in the great diVide.

There's soul there where it lies.

No room for shame from where you came.

You haVe the power of the cosmos that sits promptly between your thighs.

Let no man claim, you are rent free.

No one's property.

special V

my dreams are similar to setting a campfire.

dreams as the starter, rocks and sticks are the persistence and consistency. when they come together, at the right moment the fire is ignited. With the wind as my support, my fire roar effortlessly. my fire is grand as it lights so beautifully.

some things are better off as a once upon a time
rather than a happily ever after

boundaries

silence of voice is a fatigued solider and I refuse to be tired.

warrior

you want to peer into a woman's soul?

make her laugh.

only then will the oppressed woman rise.
the brokenhearted realigned and lightened.
the sparklein her eyes beam the room.
the air becomes lighter.
love is more cognizant.
life is majestic.

soul medicine

road trip

like the night sky blazes with darkness so does my mind. blank, not a penny drop of thoughts. this smooth, coasting ride. breeze cutting through my hair so blissfully, my hand grasping hold of the uncatchable wind.

Streetlights whim by leaving a blur.

The smooth sound of the pavement, the quiet, peaceful.

I turn to you, a star that chose to remain absent from the sky. leaving the midnight blue to join me on this midnight blue.

we are as naked as the roads with one another.

Let me make love to you. Not in a sexual state at this moment.

I want to enjoy this site of seeing you bare fully clothed.

I wish to make love to your soul. To know your deepest desires as I caress you with my fingertips and we manifest like there's no tomorrow. Let me know your deepest fears so I can help you transcend above what frightens you.

To ascend spiritually and make you cum is what enlightenment will do.

I want to make love to you through sensation with the touch of my finger, creating a ripple effect of waves making your body tremble.

Look into my eyes as I hypnotize with the bare minimum.

Sweet honey kisses that transit from my lips to yours, grip tight of my soul as this honey drips into the deep depths of your core.

With every breath in me, I wish to leave my mark of an epic journey. I know you're thinking dirty, let me remind you this is an exchange from low to high vibrational energy.

When our bodies thrust in unison from pleasure, there's no reason to be placed on a pedestal to measure.

Our souls speak loudly as we water each other's highest beings, aligning who we truly are.

You've grown quite fond of me, my dear, that's when our love begins to take us far.

Sex becomes another intimate language we learn to share.

We created a soul tie as we lay here.

Now we are naked and bare.

my apologies if I do not wish to be on the same level as I once was.

my apologies that I do not wish to club, I'd rather go on a hike and connect with Mother Earth.

I cannot fathom how people wish to remain on the same level, with the same mindset repeating same activities daily.

There's so much more to life than what is seen in this dimension.

If only people weren't afraid to actually allow themselves to venture.

my apologies for wanting to experience MY way of freedom.

She never listened to people of small minds. Their voice was unheard of. Though she knew the individual, their tongue remained foreign. As she tried to process their words, she thought her mind was too complex or she did not think simple enough.

In her heart, she knew there was more than what the small minds could say or do for her. Her body trembled as she yearned for more. Adventure lies on the tip of her tongue, exacerbated from her skin with every drip of sweat. Her soul burned with the passion to rebel against the small minds because she knew there is more that lies anywhere but here. She refused to conform with the likings of people who refused to explore.

For her, there was no such thing as coloring within the lines.

Nothing would satisfy her more than to run with the wild.

nonconformist

I allow my sadness to be here at this present moment.

Today, I grieve.

Tomorrow, I smile.

human

bend is what the world asks of us.

SO, WE BEND.

break is what love does to us.

SO, WE BREAK.

bleed is what mother nature tells us.

SO, WE BLEED.

shake is what anger utters to us.

SO, WE SHAKE.

enjoy is what sex reveal to others even against our will.

SO, WE ENJOY.

quiet is what men want from us.

SO, WE REMAIN QUIET.

HOW CAN YOU QUESTION A WOMAN'S STRENGTH WHEN WE DO ALL OF THE ABOVE???

YOU DON'T!

there comes a time where I reevaluate my space, my time given to others and time given to myself.

some call this solitude; I call it polishing my crown.

I bless my rage before releasing.

Rage is the spirit begging for peace.

Tears are the soul asking for protection, releasing out deepest anguish.

I have my father's eyes and my mother's smile, on my face they're still together. I know I am both he and she, the explanation of why I have a hard time of self-acceptance.

I am half of a person I do not know, who lost their battle to schizophrenia and I am half of a person who chooses to settle in life and become consumed by alcohol.

I wish to not let it define me, forever it will be a part of me. I choose to transcend. Acceptance of my he and she is my salvation to self acceptance.

With myself acceptance, my realization.

I am not my past.

I am not my trauma.

I am not my wound.

I choose to transcend.

transcendence

-inspiration from Warsan Shire

I am a mother.

A mother without a mother.

I thought having my own family would fill the void. I thought having motherly figures would patch this wound. I thought being a mother would complete me. But nothing can replace you. Nothing can get rid of that feeling of yearning for you. I've come to terms that I will never understand a mother's love on the receiving end. It hurts like shit, to give this adoring gift, but to remain clueless of what it feels to receive is something that will never be achieved.

Goodbye Letter to Mama

17 years of lost time and your choice to choose others remains. the universe reminded me to release resentment and gain acceptance of who you are with our last phone call.

DEAR DAD

I have traveled down a long, dry road. The wind thick with heat. Inhaling air that has been infused with fumes lit with fire finding it hard to breathe.

The sun scorching and no one there to turn it off. I'm drenched in black clothing making it harder for myself. Not knowing I made that decision but not one time did I question myself why the hell do I continue to wear black. I'm at a stop. It tells me to drop the load here. I keep walking. Every year I pass the same sign. "Drop load here." I keep walking.

The 28th year rolls around. I realize I'm walking in a circle, seeing the sign "drop load here." Back aching, mind shattering with pain. I finally decide to drop the load, and continue to walk. I see a bench with white clothes, and an umbrella. I remove the black and replace them with the white clothing. I'm feeling breezy. The wind feels cooler and lighter, I continue to walk. I see water. I take a sip, refreshed. I water myself. I come to a fork in the road that was once invisible. I'm wondering why the hell I've never seen this road before. I never noticed because I made it harder for myself to see differently while holding onto baggage that wasn't mine to keep.

I have carried my burdens well.

I have carried my mama's burdens well.

I have carried my father's burdens well.

Now I choose to walk on and water myself.

16 is my beautiful number.

Last night I had a dream about you, my heart still hurts. The pain descended to my gut fucking with my self-confidence, weakening my foundation of who I am, my awareness. The pain ascends, causing me to refrain from saying the things I want to truly express, allowing negativity to make itself home within my temple. I allowed people to run over me, running through lovers looking for something you were supposed to bring forth within me. You were supposed to help me discover me. And because I think so, not only is my anger towards you, my dispute is also with the universe.

"Please universe, God, let me show you how my life was supposed to go because you didn't do it right." My way of thinking caused me suffocation; a decade passes. Add the number 6 to that of a long battle of self-sabotage.

Now it is different, I know I will never beat the universe, I let go of the control I wished have. While doing so, my load is lighter, my world is brighter. I am grateful for the years of turmoil. I'm beginning to understand my journey. My pain resides but it no longer has power over me. Acceptance shall reign.

16 will always remain my beautiful number.

16

commitments

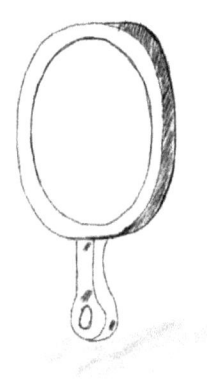

to self….

This journey of healing is about you, a time to come back to your authentic self, releasing what no longer serves you. Do not use this sacred time concerning yourself of what others are thinking of you or what he or she is doing with their time.

This is about YOU.

Commitment 1

Romanticize YOUR life.

No one can love you like you. Be your own vibe, be THE innerG you want to attract.

Visualize and realize how beautiful everything in your life already is, how the pain you've endured was the exact chaos you need/needed to discover the true beauty of you.

Widen that tunnel vision just far enough and watch how everything reveals itself. Take yourself on dates, dance, have moments where you talk to yourself in the mirror like Issa. You're not crazy, you're just getting know you.

Make that commitment to yourself and keep it.

I've always frowned upon romance.

I grew fond of romance once I learned to love myself.

Romance is love

    love is liberation

        liberation is what we all crave for and seek.

Commitment 2

There are many types of love and different ways of loving.

love yourself in all of those many types and ways before

loving someone else.

Liberation that is shackled and residing in

darkness becomes the brightest to shine once broken free.

Commitment 3

Living in the present is the bravest act of self love.

Put all of your being in that moment.

The past doesn't have a hold on you asking to be resolved.

The future isn't asked to be seen or thought of.

The present requires you to trust and love yourself in confidence through any emotion and experience.

Be brave and live in the now.

<u>Commitment 4</u>

REMINDER:

Sleep is luxurious, pamper yourself with rest

Commitment 5

Your energy is your currency.

You have every right to take every part of yourself you gave to others and places back and transform it into something greater.

You break, how you break.

You look inward, prioritize, focus, and improve at your own pace,

HEAL (do not rush the process)

HEAL AGAIN (this is not going to happen in 3 months)

HEAL AGAIN.

Before you know it, you've moved on.

Jealousy housed my lack of confidence.

I had to BURN it down.

I change with the seasons.

I stand out or I choose to blend where I see fit rapidly shifting like a chameleon.

I'm a wanderer that constantly wonders a life of stability,
    the white picket fence a grand garden in back.

Knowing my life will be filled in awe of boredom trying to get instability back.

Inconsistency is anything but foreign to me, in fact it's paradise.

Why settle for steady when life is all about taking chances and rolling the dice?

Commitment 6

The only validation I seek is from myself.

Commitment 7

AFFIRMATION:

I create space for my personal peace.

<u>Commitment 8</u>

Bare minimum... HA!

   what is that?!

      Love yourself enough to soar above the bare minimum

Commitment 9

Remember what an honor it is to live your life.

No one can live your life the way you can.

Grasp every moment and feel it.

There's beauty in that moment.

Luxury to me is waking up and living my life at a steady pace. Everything is serene…

>from the music in my background,
>>to the cool water splashing my plush skin.

>The cottons and silks that snug my body or hang loosely allowing my body to breathe.

>I am the main character of this story that I choose to create on a daily basis.

Commitment 10

Forgive yourself and love yourself gently.

Leaving all known things to elevate is tough.

With elevation, I carry those sweet memories of those nights I wish I can do over. The familiar faces that bring fun and comfort.

Those places I visited where I wish I could have 5 more minutes to just be. I have to leave a piece of myself to gain a piece of a newer me.

Clearing the path for room for improvement.
Somewhat of Spring cleaning.
Familiar is home that the spirit won't allow me to settle.

I came back to this life as a wanderer always traveling into the unknown.

When I choose the familiar, my life becomes foreign.

When I choose foreign, my life becomes familiar.

Those who choose to explore and elevate are one of the many brave.

Commitment 11

I love myself enough to not torture myself of negative thoughts of the past. Those thoughts no longer serve me.
I love being in a loving, healthy relationship with myself.

There are three perspectives: the way you view yourself, the way others view you, and who you really are.

Which perspective matters to you?

Choose wisely.

Commitment 12

Instead of complaining,

change it,

release it,

elevate.

Do what you need to do, just don't complain.

You can rewrite your story at any time.

Motherhood Affirmations

I handle one cry at a time.
I handle one mommy at a time.
I handle one expression of one's emotions at a time.
I handle one child at a time.
I pace through motherhood with patience.
I have patience with myself and my emotions
I have patience with my child.
I have patience with my children.
I accept my role in my child's life and their roles in mine.
I accept that I am doing the best I can.
I pace through motherhood with patience.
I am learning from my child just as much as I teach them.
I am learning from my children just as much as I teach them.
I am raising my little person the best way I know how.
I am open minded when it comes to parenting.
I am always open to discovering what works for me and my child.
I pace through motherhood with patience.
I am learning myself again.
I am important.
I am a priority.
My well-being matters.
I make time for self-care.
I love myself.

        For those hard days…

Commitment 13

Admire both strengths and weaknesses about yourself.

You are constantly learning both from life experiences which inspires growth.

And that itself is beautiful.

I don't respect the person you were, making it hard to love you in the now.

I've healed too much to still be in love with you as the unhealed me would be.

The you now is asking for a chance, approaching with a fresh start.

A new love.

It is the old you that survives in my head, letting me know that I don't need a new you.
I need to experience something new without you.

Loving myself correctly first will lead me to accepting the correct love for me.

My inner masculine won't rest until it knows WE are safe; if you never experience my feminine, you have yourself to blame.

when i accepted you for who you are instead of who i thought you to be,

    i had to love you different and i had to love me more.

I'm uncomfortable in this relationship.

I forgave you.

I thought once forgiveness sat in, I would be comfortable.

I would feel safe.

But somehow discomfort remains, it's eating me alive.

To be here with you, every second, is to leave myself.

I can't concur.

I've become a blur.

Losing myself, no longer to you, but to who I used to be.

I'm not the girl that tolerates disrespect.
I'm not the girl that thinks she can save you.
I'm not the girl that's waiting for you to understand my love language.

I am the woman that leaves at an inch of disrespect.
I am the woman that saves herself.
I am the woman that loves herself and creates languages of love for herself.

This is a me season.

My time is valuable,
my words stand with meaning,
my confidence is on that high horse, that I have don't have to be loud because
my ethereal presence draws in a crowd.

Baby I'm flourishing.

There's no way in hell I can reward your disloyalty by staying.

I am the greatest love of my life.

I am my own epic love story.

I don't depend on man for an epic tale of true, fantasized love or a romantic love.

I prefer man to be gentle with me, yes. I prefer man to caress me with pleasure, yes. I prefer man to share a story with a time or dozen, yes. Man plays a small part of my love story.

But man does not lie in this skin, man does not take care of this vessel, man does not think my thoughts or train them to say good things to me.

Man does not see my flaws and learn to love them even on those days when loving these flaws aren't linear. Man can love someone else greater than himself or me while lying in me.

I am the great love of this epic tale of romance. The stars of my birth right told me so. Another lifetime ago, I believe I loved man before me. I came back with the same thought, wanting to be loved desperately by he. Until he broke me time and time again, in different bodies, with different laughs and quirks. But each body be familiar spirit. He broke me because I didn't fix me.

I myself am my own love story. My love for me isn't linear either, but it's far greater to give myself the power to love me better than anyone could.

Commitment 14

The many times I've had to mother and celebrate myself,

I'll never again allow someone else to take my power.

Commitment 15

My love for me knows boundaries.

My love for me knows when to walk away.

My love for me knows any hurt from others does not begin with me, but with them.

My love for me has no room for victim mentality.

My love for me pushes fear out.

My love for me only allows those who make me feel good in honor of my space.

My love for me will never bring me harm, only peace.

Negative projection from them requires major protection for you.

Commitment 16

REMINDER:

Don't repeat that toxic cycle because you're bored. You're wanting to look back because it's familiar and somewhat a safety net.

You're doing great by moving forward.

Keep going.

Commitment 17

REMINDER:

On the brink of elevation, you may begin to miss the familiar.

The familiar is safe, but the unknown has greater in store. Keep pushing yourself out of your comfort zone.

You got this.

Commitment 18

Slow down. Love slow. I've always loved fast, being afraid that if i didn't love fast enough they would speed off.

I learn to take things slow. Pace easily with everything.

Everything that is for me, is already mine.

Rest, Reset, Reflection

The goal is growth.

You are allowed to become a better, different version of yourself.

affirmations

Acceptance is a gift, a breath of fresh air.

You cannot change the past; it is best to not dwell on it. You cannot change what happened two seconds ago as you read the previous lines.

Whatever that has happened to cause you to be where you are, understand that you could have not gone through to be here in this present moment. Disregard the memories that may be horrific, for they do not define who you are.

You are aiming for a better direction.

Use the heartache, pain to embrace you into your truest self. May it direct you to love, light, and positivity to spread to your peers and those closest to you.

Accept your past, but allow it to bring you home.

acceptance

manifesting ideas is becoming one with spirit and soul.

Comparison kills confidence.

Jealousy fuels anger.

You are good enough, you are beautiful.

Do not find your ways by looking at others and their ways.

Your ways are just as glorious.

You are unique in your own way.

Don't let anyone take that away from you.

The truest form of hate is fear.

Hate is not hate.

When you hate someone, you fear them.

Fear cannot overcome love.

Love can never be defeated.

Love drives out fear. Fear can NEVER win.

If you believe fear can surpass love, then you do not know God.

love reigns

I fit on this garden we call Earth so naturally,

the birds and the bees sing to me.

To see a fellow flower, that is to see me grown so beautifully.

The ones that are misfortunate and ungrateful

are the ones that do not belong here.

if I were in a room filled with everyone I've ever fell in love with.

I'd choose me.

loving myself

Protect your energy.

When you are transcending to a higher frequency,
the universe may test you to reveal your true strength.

Today I realized that my life is mine. No one belongs to me; therefore, nothing shall have control over me. Why do I linger onto what I already know?

Why do I let things bother me? I cannot control things that are out of my control.

I am not God, though God is within me.

I know people that I have chosen to play a role in my life. I know how they maneuver based on the past, present and their present. I know what they are capable of but it is up to me to deal with it. I ask myself these questions...

Do their actions display something within my nature?

Is the love I give, returned to me in a healthy state?

Do I allow their actions to dictate my emotions?

Do I allow people to have a hold on me?

I realize I know my love and I love it.

I refuse to allow people to snatch my love, my confidence, my joy from me.

This is mine, my spirit. This is mine!

Mine

Today I let go of things that I allow to make myself feel inferior of others

Today I let go of self-doubt and uncertainty within myself

Today I let go of envy, for I am as beautiful as God created me to be.

I am divine.

Today I let go of who I was and embrace who I am now in this moment, in this time and space.

Today I let go of the past and its burdens, though the events have taken place, they do not define me, but mold me into a better me.

Today I let go of everything that I am not and accept everything that I am.

I breathe.

I let go.

Let nothing define you.

You are your own woman.

No job, no title, no status could ever define your being.

Steer away from trying to control a situation because one thing is out of your control.

Come back to you.

Don't doubt yourself because the unknown has surfaced.

Don't doubt your being.

The universe won't be against you if you flow along with it.

I admire you as I see you in your purest form as your true self. Grounded in who you are, your spirit dances with life.

"I am"

I admire your curiosity of what attracts you. Though you haven't fully discovered your deepest desires. You dive into the desires of now.

"I feel"

I admire your impulsiveness. Everything is so natural, your playfulness, your sway. You remain dauntless.

"I do"

Guided by your intuition, you give love when you feel that it is reciprocated and when needed. You withdraw and distance yourself when feel that it isn't true.

"I love"

I admire your tenacity and wit. Fearless with expressing your emotions. Unafraid to tell people how you feel.

"I speak"

Unknowing of the what the world actually holds, but with the wakening of your third eye you are aware.

I admire your innocence. So simple and sweet.

"I see"

You envision your crown; by your sight it isn't invisible. Your stance lies in a state of bliss.

" I understand"

chakra mantras

AFFIRMATION:

I AM CREATIVE

My creative juices are exploding.

I create with my fingertips, with pen and paper, or brushes of paint and that of a canvas. With pen and paper, my words appear breaking down every feeling my spirit presents.

When I create my spirit speaks, my soul shouts. Leaping for joy...the fire is ignited as the wheels within my cranium begin to turn.

When I create....

I can feel the vibrations of my frequency lifting higher causing the ancestors to rejoice and dance.

My creation...........is me taking back my power.

My creation...........is my soul speaking to others, the ego remains absent.

My creation....is my spirt revealing the magic within me whether others can relate or not for the world to understand or myself to seek validation from others.

My creation is myself acceptance allowing me to be free of the tremors of this world, handing me the key to unlocking the doors of the outer world.

I welcome anew.

My creations are my peace, my eternal bliss.

That I choose to share with the world.

A part of myself I give freely to the world.

My creativity possesses joy.

My creativity possesses peace.

My creativity possesses love

I am creative.

I am creative.

I am creative.

DIVINE AFFIRMATIONS

I am divine.
I am a money magnet.
I am all things above and beyond. I am the gift and the curse.
cursed by the blessings to become the chosen one.
gift as I am gifted by my God and ancestors. I am the bundled gift wrapped in skin; my crown be my big red ribboned bow. When I am unraveled, my gift shines as bright. My gift shines bright like the north star that led my ancestors to what came to be, a breath of fresh air.
My gift is the north star, leading those to a new way of life, a new of perception.

this gift. the luxury of being me. to choose this vessel to experience this life. without a doubt, everything is aligned. just for me.

love fearlessly.

live free.

enjoy the ride.

I am my ancestors. I am living for them and myself as they live through me.

Reconciling with my past!

Fear of anything is nonexistent

Fear of anything is nonexistent

I am to live in the present moment.

Love wholly, rest beautifully and fearlessly.

I am my ancestors.

I am healing my family lineage by being me. I am healing others through life itself.

I am love.

I am life.

I am woman.

I am God.

I am a Goddess.

I manifest.

I create.

I rebel.

I am wild, free, and forever young

AFFIRMATION:

I love myself.

-January 29, 2021 (the day I actually meant it.)

odes

Dawn began to crack. Her bare feet stepped onto the cool, dew grass. Her eyelids closed. She stretched her neck back to feel the crisp wind traveling downward, like a crane grasping at its feathers. She inhaled deeply, and exhaled with satisfaction.

She is connected one with Mother Nature, with God.

"I can feel you pulling me away. With every puff I take of my cigarette, the taste becomes sickening. With every tale of gossip that enters my ear, and that rolls off my tongue, I become disappointed with myself. The things that are limited within this world are becoming subdued. I've lost interest. Everything that is within this earthly realm is so bland, it isn't me.

My spirit, my true self is trying to excel beyond who and where I am right now, but my earthly self is resisting. I know I can never run away from You for I know my steps are directed by You, how can I understand my own way? I cannot combat with You; I will never win.

Just take over. Let Your spirit rule me just as You rule the worlds. Uplift me just as nature does my inner being, liberate me from every burden that I choose not to relinquish, carry me just as the wind carries a small piece of lint. Take me Almighty One for I am Yours to take."

Ase

golden hour/ sun dancer

- An Ode to God I

Your laughter, your gibberish. Your smile, your perfect face.

Your gleaming eyes light up my darkest days.

No one can take your face from my memory.

You are my home, just I am yours.

Give yourself permission to bloom where you are planted. Know your roots and remain solid in them but have the courage and knowledge to know that you are mobile.

Never hinder yourself my sweet, always choose yourself, be true to you. And if you shall lose yourself, rediscover yourself until you have found your soul to be home again.

- An Ode to my Daughters

I ask myself how could I lose hope in you?

How could I not believe that you would rescue me time after time again?

How could I even think that you would let me fall and not pick me up when You are the only one that understands my true being?

You know me better than I know myself, you've given me the ability to choose to be myself or to be like the person the world idolizes. When I choose to be as of the world, you still love me the same just as I choose to be more like You. You never left me and You never will.

Though many of us are living lucidly, we wait for the day when it is time for You to wake us from this lucid dream. We will meet each other and You will give us a play back of the person we chose to be in the dream you allowed us to experience. You will then reveal to most of us that do not know that our life was just a dream.

- An Ode to God II

About the Author

Jennifer Harris was born on June 20, 1992, in Birmingham, Alabama. Jennifer began writing at the age of 9, but later put down her pen while trying to explore other ventures. Birthed from a mother who suffered from schizophrenia and a father who suffered with alcoholism, decided her her roots would not define her, but mold her to beginning a new found way of living to honor her lineage. She has a children's book series and a thriller novel in the works.

Published Works:

What About Me?!!

www.ingramcontent.com/pod-product-compliance
Lightning Source LLC
Chambersburg PA
CBHW051605010526
44119CB00056B/793